CH01394943

VOT

Also by Keiran Goddard

STRINGS
FOR THE CHORUS

Votive

~

KEIRAN GODDARD

First published in 2019
by Offord Road Books

offordroadbooks.co.uk
@OffordRoadBooks

Typeset by Offord Road Books
Printed in the UK by TJ International

All rights reserved © Keiran Goddard, 2019

The right of Keiran Goddard to be identified as author
of this work is asserted in accordance with Section 77
of the Copyrights, Designs and Patents Act 1988

ISBN 978-1-9999304-8-6

1 3 5 7 9 10 8 6 4 2

O•R•B

'The sea is not less beautiful in our eyes because we know that sometimes ships are wrecked by it.'

— SIMONE WEIL, *Waiting On God*

~

I   St Aldates Church, Oxford   3

II   St Patrick's Church, Toronto   25

III   St Pancras Church, London   45

St Aldates Church, Oxford

~

Candles in the vaulting light of it
and the heat of it too
and do they blow them out at closing?
Yes, yes I suppose they do . . .

It was the finer
than light

light
that we rose to

the enough
flame to suck

down enough
of the match

that struck us
too little

to trade
for this life

for the spring
of the sea

in the pulse
of our skulls

for the four sets
of bone

that are
patiently honed

into sickling
blades

by a sharp
oystershell

they're protectors
we said

until the bone
turns to wax

until the candle
is gone

and the light
and the match

The day has come to estimate our loss.
For a start, there's our tongues,
the muscles we use
for breaking the food.

There's the short-wave hiss
of wine on the lip
as it summons our blood
with the promise of gold.

There's the hummingbird sketch
that we held of this life,
made relentless and proud
by the scratch of the ink.

And there's the ruck of your dress
landing slick on the waist,
the scintilla, the numinous,
the symbol, the paint.

Our hope that night
had a hand-me-down look,
begging for stitching;
it was rain-washed, in need.

So we aimed with intent
and we threaded the needle,
our hands glossed with sweat
as we forced through our point.

In these solitary months
we're starched cold with obedience,
wishing for nights full
of fattening sleep.

We whisper that blizzards
don't feed as they pass,
but that mists come with hunger
for hope and for shame.

Ask what can we promise
to this star getting colder,
split nerves in our home
and split nerves in the wild

and it ends with our camera's
pellucid new cry,
Your hatchling is dead . . .
but bring worms, feed the child!

You've a bonsai body
planted off-centre.
I broke you like that
to leave space
for the gods.

But they still never come –
stand straight!
lock the bolt!
I need your legs now
and I need them like tusks.

You built it
with sealing wax
and petty grace
but took to the sea
unprepared for its roiling.

It brought algal bloom
and blackening fish
which to prove
they had lived
came reaching for land.

But you had appetite still
for a belly of salt
enriched for a time
and then bloating
to burst.

And you remember this now
as a life at its fullest
a commandment to drink
tongue the brine
slay the thirst.

I dream of powder,
or possibly ash,
granular things
that flow freely when touched.

I relish the work of scooping
and holding,
of watching the wind
turn it over with ease.

I see it configure
itself and then rise,
and then numberless things
fall back to their place.

Your voice had
the minatory torque
of the intensely
familiar
because you came
from wherever
teenagers came from
in every
1980s film
that pretended to be
about martial arts
but was actually about
missing your dad.

What my blood felt mattered,
and back then it clung
to the half-dark of home
with the rapture
of a dancer,
who sensing
the light as it left
entered the parade,
weighed his love
and found it wanting
against the steady
thrum of the ballroom.

We were graceless and rapt
but were witness
so watched
as love breathed in
and offered
its neck to our teeth.

And starving
we chewed
with blank
empty greed
snagging its skin
as the two of us ate

until dervish
and sated
we let the rest
of it spoil
to an occasional twitch
and the last of its heat.

something sacred
a watermark
a vow
and a votive light
something mewling for meat
something unflinching
something ungoverned
incarnate
something blink and bloom
and tiller and mainsail

In a russet cloak
of wet branch
the river sought home,
and finding home
found warmth
that plumed
at the flesh
and into the bone,
of tin
of iron
of black diamond dust,
and there
our hopes grew
reforged,
remade
in the life-cry of blood
and the death-song of rust.

By common consent
a new hush
rose over Europe.

You welcomed it
with your mouth full
of tuning pegs

slid a gnarl
of blue lace
down your thighs

and mopped the floor
clean of the heaven
you'd made.

There is nothing
we can know
well enough
to dwarf
the livid shock
of our fantasies
ageing.

Or the patched
cauterised
paint of a home
once gravid
defiant
but now peeling
in tides.

If you stay awhile
I will command
these continents
into wiser shapes.

I will make a ladder
of lean limbs
and redraw the map
as our slow compensation.

It is the first morning
the window
letting through
enough light
to show the dirt
of Oxford brick
and show everything
I have ever seen
or known
piled up and swaying
in corners
every white shirt
every statue and rock
every person, pencil
spoon and black shoe
and all of the beaten gold
I ever folded and shaped.
I will guard it all
sentinelling
and never sleeping
and I will die
scabrous with hope.

I stopped short
pressed my face
into the scrubbed clean
and twisted sky

felt myself as ruthless
and as summoned

St Patrick's Church, Toronto

~

You solemnly swear
to peel back the bandage
and let all of my pollen lift.

With clean hands you work
the blue-gold pelt of me
until I am just soft enough to split.

You reach in and search
for the simple dead things,
old muscle and tissue and bone.

Then you drink all your fill,
sew and then bathe me,
and tie up the thread at the end of the wound.

You count down from twenty
then untangle the knot,
and tear me again where the grace of this bloomed.

The giving of things appears
with its own formality
the precise unstringing
of its armour
(the leaf, the wet vine)
and the discarding of those
in a place they won't grow
but as they tear at this gift
my fingers stay hidden
they are peeling back calyx
to seek something ungreen.

That night, we hovered
for hours on the
very edge of touch

*I'm using my left hand
to restrain my right*

That night, you looked
dressed in river
dancing in your chair

*this is the single best
thing I have ever known*

That night, you were
a universe unfolding
from inside of a matchbox

*I've decided, if I die
I want you to claim me*

As you run
through flitting shards
of hardened rain
I catch the glint
of last summer
tight in your fist
like a blade

A hailstorm
of names

that are always
your name

held now
as praise-song

as harmony
and pitch

all open
all empty

no rafters
no crowd

repetition
and reflex

and ineffable
sound.

Sing it smaller
sing it briefer
the omen song
of your body
shivering in bed
like a new root
working its way into soil.

Where the ground lipped
the rabbits lived,
the dog hid the carrion
behind pet shops and bars.

It would pluck them up
by the sweep of their thighbone,
the world turning silver
as the glare caught their eyes.

They would hang like a lantern
in the grip of its maw,
two lumbering lights
made to mark the way home.

After scraping the rapture
from our tongues
we watched for our future
as it grew under glass

stayed silent as detail
set and then fused
a fingernail forced
into the dark of a fist.

To get purchase for paring
you trench the orange with your teeth
place a nail in its groove
and uncoil its twisted skin.

I watch the peel as it pools
in the lap of your dress
reading as coastline
come to rest against sea.

When I say this
you tell me the dress isn't blue
but I'm so sure of the light
and of my turning toward you.

At my father's funeral
I set an early alarm
and shoulder my dead
to prove he had lived.
I lift the thick-bodied man
(the type, like me, that you measure in hands)
and meet the howl of the horse
as the bullet breaks in;
I take this man of his word
to the hole he has made
and I harden to courage
as the song of him ends;
I press my face to his flank, ask
what do I need when I'm scattered?
and then I ask him again
what do I need in defeat?

I give myself the talking to:
cup your hands son
pull back form slouch
cough up your excuse like a man

hack up its weight
spit from the lip of the bank
and watch as it floats
right past you on foam

peel back truth's heft
like a sweated-on vest
and be sure to down tools
before the last job is done.

I have one single
measured task

to steward regret
like a splinted relic
that I am in charge
of returning

I cannot miss it
it is a carving
of a thin red bird

braided about
its folded wing
with hair

I must return it
whole to the devoted

bear the leanness
that comes
with the journey

lay the red bird down
under cover
of darkness

and let the bird be there
when the devoted
they rise.

I thumb
open the bird's beak,
press long enough
that the old glue
flints from the edges
and its runic curl
releases
a shorthand prayer:

you cannot make me home
you cannot make me home

The moth knocks
against my hand

survival music
keeping steady time.

I cannot approve
of all this dying

I need to see it lift
and in its greying light
see the last candle left.

The prim mathematics
of a handkerchief
like a still boat
on the lip of a pocket

an era about to untie itself
white rain of new sun
something once slow
about to get quicker . . .

Toronto flinched
heaved its weight
onto the horizon
and coughed out
a ribbon of blood

Intent on its dying
you gripped at its ribs
sank it airless
and whole
back under the ice.

Unrelenting you tied
the things to the things,
made me weigher,
herder and trader of hope.

I stood holding your lines
until my voice just gave out,
to my senile bark
and my wavering note.

It is nearing the end
of our fallen year

and it feels like we are
watching ourselves live.

St Pancras Church, London

~

Two years
of knowing you
has made
me an animal
that actively expects
to live
and through your
unlyrical
eloquence
I have learnt
there is always
a path
from the rocks
to the sea.

We can no longer be
scholars of bright light.

I read the runes
of your daughter's hair
unbound, untied
risking the cliffs of her shoulder,
splayed and dry
as a paintbrush
pressed on blank paper,
speaking but speaking
unsure,
unsteady,
a childhood script
unpractised in summer.

You knock
your tongue
against my guts
and hiss

you are entirely made
from the parts of the sea
that the sea didn't want

London was the type
of bright that felt
conclusive, correct,
pelting white sky in sheets.

If not a sign of new faith
then what? Mischance?
a thick mass of watchmen
kicking their boots?

It drew a clear line
around our grace,
and then it left, and then it left
all of its marks, accordingly.

The new sacrament
felt unfamiliar,
squat with intent
in the curve of my hand

and its arrogant gaze
at the white meat of things
made me gasp like a fish
being wrenched onto land.

Unnerved, I searched life
for patterns and peace,
found nothing but splinter
come pushing at palm

but in time, time resumed me
unhooked me, made raw
until exhausted I lived
in the grip of its calm.

I must remember
to consult
the pillowcase
for the day's
collected rain
and churn it
for an hour
in my cheeks
and spend
the rest
of my relapse
in a gallery
or cinema
trying to die
with something
that at least
approaches
a formal grace.

I nag myself in psalms
and they end in accusation;
You are a nothing but
a bronchial weak-chested boy
a shrewd-eyed swindler
spittle-chinned and unfit
to dust this snuff
from your Sunday best,
may God speak
and let all of your chickens die.

Again I wake with blood
crusting the corner of my gum –
in sleep I had thought it
clear water, fresh bread
or fruit.

Picking it clean I release
a red-black river
running flush on smooth cliffs,
a single flame
passed between two candles.

Frame this
several times over:
this erratic machine
unclipped
undressed
fucking to the howl
of an old alarm clock.

Can you hear that call?
It's our childless future –

evenings of circular fetish
whole weeks left in ruin

so open your dress
let's begin things again –

we are hungry for movement
and mercy and food.

You insisted
that old bone
always looks clean
and untarnished

that if you went grabbing at earth
you'd emerge
from the dirt
with scraps of light in your grip.

That you'd curve them like soap
in the bowl of your palm,
then straighten them out
and return them to rest.

You were certain you said
that's how diamonds are made,
by two desperate hands
raking sod for the gleam.

Can we drag this pain out
into crooked light

and hang it like a rabbit
salted for winter?

We can fence it off
and ready the fire

there is nothing left here
we can't use for fuel.

I lay
in the arms
of that bar
spread sober
and ready
as a new nail.

I seemed
a mad strong
pliant bird
who fell prey
to bright cloth
and to moonshine.

I refused to see
the legible end

when the corkscrew
stopped drilling
and settled to rest

and stopped mauling
glass gullet
for the bloom of its wine.

She lay
sliding
a scalpel
on the map
of my back
and the pieces
she took?
well, they hunt me
in packs.

The loose
high-hat rhythm
of car keys on coffee table,
that daily song,
that top-line shuffle
of endless return.

As things now stand
in all of their
rapt unlikeliness
I can just make out
a new horizon
and though
the light
is weak
and worsening
its almost-gold
is almost certain
and I know it
from the crack
of this rain
as it lands.

There's an
awful lot
of time
now you're gone

I buy
counterfeit Van Dycks
for a home
I don't have

then draw in biro
every soldier
who got honoured
for their bravery

I start a family
incantate in bars
about the state
of labour markets

drink enough coffee
that I shake
and start to find
fountains beautiful

I could admit
I'm a coward
and start speaking
more plainly

or just paint this
and dry this
and watch this
and wait.

Astonished is a word
I will slowly learn
to use again without guilt

and I will learn to confess
that the steam of your skin
makes me pedant and hoarder and clerk.

I will be unembarrassed
that this density of breath
feels like something to salvage

that it hits like the swelter
of a boundless summer
spent unwarping wood in the silence of heat.

In prayer I will remember
that the strong upward reel of you
taught me that I was ecstatic

and that it sang my every excess,
and that I could not turn away,
and that I could not turn away.

Acknowledgements

~

Not a single one of these poems has appeared in print anywhere before. For that reason, among many others, I am especially thankful to Martha Sprackland and Hannah Williams at Offord Road Books for their belief in the book, and the vision and editorial skill they have exhibited throughout.

Thanks are due to the University of Cambridge and the University of Reading, who hosted me at various points during the writing of this book.

I also offer thanks and love to my family and to Olivia Chambers, for their unwavering support, to Matthew Green and Eugenia Zuroski for their particularly close involvement in the work, and to Luke Brown, Emmie Francis, Anna Kelly, Ed Lake, Lucy Luck and Imogen Pelham for their utterly necessary diversions.